Myth Busting 2
Thai Women Are
All the Same

Myth-Busting 3
High-Value Thai
Women Are
Unattainable

Myth Busting 4
Thai Women Are
Only Interested in
Wealth

Myth-Busting 5
Dating Thai Girls Is
Only for Casual fun

Do & Don't of
Approaching
Thai Girls

Sustaining
Passion and
a Healthy
Relationship
with a Thai
Girl

Myth-Busting 6
Thai Women Are
Submissive

Marriage Law/Visa,
Lawsuit Against
Adultery, Property
Ownership as a
Foreigner, and
Retirement

Hello I'm

Dr. Dada

Lecturer: Teaching English/Teaching Thai
for Foreigners Interest: English for Healthy
Relationship/Cross-cultural Communication

Working as an English language teacher at a Thai university for over 15 years has given me the opportunity to see firsthand the complex dynamics of human relationships and cross-cultural communication. The need for cultural sensitivity and effective communication in building healthy relationships is something I've learned from experience.

Throughout my career, I've made it my personal goal to help promote cross-cultural understanding, strengthen relationships, and reduce language and cultural barriers. I gained accreditation for teaching Thai to non-native speakers after being motivated to study more about the complexities of intercultural communication by my enthusiasm for language teaching. These experiences have taught me much about the challenges of intercultural relationships, especially those between men from other cultures and women raised in Thailand.

With this book, "Break the Myths That: Successfully Dating High-Value Thai Girls," I hope to empower foreign men by sharing my insights, knowledge, and experiences in order to help them overcome the difficulties of dating and build healthy relationships with Thai women. I wish to refute popular beliefs and prejudices regarding Thai women and offer helpful advice on building healthy relationships based on mutual respect, understanding, and appreciation. I do this by drawing on my years of teaching experience and cross-cultural interactions.

My ultimate goal is to promote clear communication, empathy, and cultural awareness in order to encourage committed relationships between foreign men and Thai women.

Warm regards, Dada

BREAK
THE
MYTH'S THAT

FOR SUCCESSFULLY DATING HIGH-VALUE THAI GIRLS

A FOREIGNER'S GUIDE TO BUILDING CONNECTIONS AND COMMITMENT

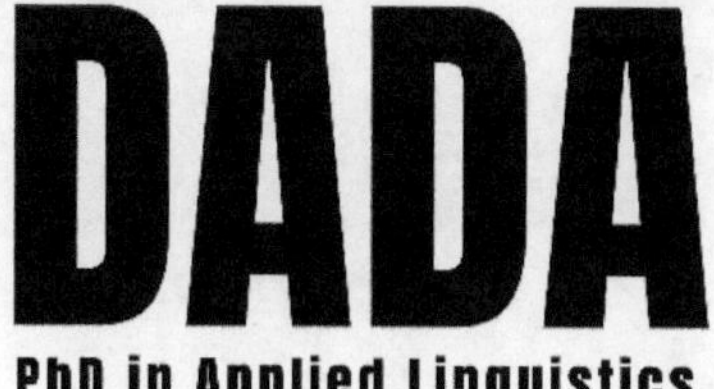

PhD in Applied Linguistics

จัดทำโดย Dr.Dada

ISBN 978-616-612-274-9

TABLE OF CONTENTS

MYTH-BUSTING 1 CULTURAL DIFFERENCES ARE INSURMOUNTABLE:

FINDING COMMON GROUND AND UNDERSTANDING

Cultural features and traditions have an immense impact on how people in Thailand link with each other and form relationships. These customs are a result of ideas, habits, and social rules that have been around for a long time and have grown over time. To get along with Thai society, it's necessary to learn about and accept these differences.

Buddhism is a main component of Thai culture and permeates many aspects of Thai daily life. It's essential to be kind, sensitive, and aware of Buddhism, as they help you get along with other people. Thai people honor adults, monks, and religious rituals because Buddhist principles have impacted the way individuals act in society. Thai society places great importance on family values, emphasizing the ideals of filial care and kin love. In Thailand, the family is the most important thing in life. It gives people a sense of identity, safety, and support. (Kuppako, 2014)

Many Thai people find it's very important to respect parents and seniors. Families view family get-togethers and parties as opportunities to preserve traditions and strengthen family bonds. In Thai culture, too, formal systems are very essential, especially when it comes to how people communicate with each other and how society functions. Elders, authorities, and those in higher positions deserve respect due to their authority and social standing. This hierarchical mindset affects people's communication styles, social interactions, and decision-making processes. It also shapes people's relationships with one another in a variety of situations. (Tomasetto et al., 2011)

Important Cultural Customs and Values to be Mindful of When Dating Thai Women

You may discover that you need to adjust to their beliefs and traditions, which are different from your own. Western men who want to attract and keep Thai women must become familiar with the basic characteristics of Thai society.

1. Respecting Elders and Other Authority Figures

Traditional Thai traditions incorporate respect for one's elders and those in positions of authority. Thai girls have traditionally learned to respect and follow the guidance of their parents and other elders. Men from the West would do well to keep in mind this traditional practice and treat their Thai partners' families and elderly with the respect they deserve.

2. The Importance of Families

Thai girls place great importance on their families, often fostering close relationships with them. Family obligations and decisions may have an impact on their dating choices, as well as the dynamics of their relationships. Western men should be ready to interact with their Thai partner's family, showing sincere curiosity and respect for their customs and beliefs.

3. Courtesies and Empathy

Thai girls generally value modesty and politeness in social situations. They may communicate more subtly and indirectly than Western women. Western men should be patient and understanding of Thai girls' unique communication styles, avoiding acting aggressively or approaching them directly.

4. Sensitivity to Variations in Culture

Being sensitive to cultural differences is important when dating Thai women. Western males must refrain from any actions or words that could potentially offend Thai culture. Understanding local norms and customs, such as respecting objects of worship and refraining from public displays of affection, can make dates more comfortable for Western males.

5. Gender Roles

Traditionally, women in Thailand are expected to conform to the gender role expectation of being the good wife. This refers to the traditional expectation for women to stay home and take care of the children and household duties while men are the only breadwinners in the family (Remya & Arasu, 2017).

6. Saving Face

In Thai culture, social harmony and "saving face" are highly valued concepts. (Punjaroje & Morrison, 2007) Thai girls may avoid confrontation or conflict in order to maintain their social status and avoid looking foolish. Thai women have the right to feel respected, so Western men should avoid doing anything that could make them appear foolish or uncomfortable in public.

In conclusion, Western males dating Thai women should understand the basic cultural norms and practices. If Western men can build powerful connections with Thai women based on shared respect and knowledge of their culture if they are receptive, respectful, and culturally understanding.

Expectations and Gender Roles

Thai society's gender roles are considerably influenced by deep-rooted cultural norms and beliefs. In Thai culture, these roles set standards for the social roles, responsibilities, and expected acts of men and women.

As the head of the household, men in Thai society are responsible for making important decisions that affect the family, career, and finances. We also expect men to possess qualities such as assertiveness, decisiveness, and strength. However, society typically expects women to fulfill more traditional roles at home. They are usually in charge of the family's care, nurturing, and housekeeping. Women should also exhibit qualities such as compassion, quietness, and submission. (Remya & Arasu, 2017). The previous study (Sodha, Özbilgin, and Connolly, 2010) found that the traditional position of women in Thai families hinders their professional aspirations, and the male-dominated society has a similar effect on women's opportunities for academic and professional success. These factors may contribute to Thailand's gender disparity.

However, the shift to modernity in Thailand has changed this gender role expectation due to the demand for a higher living standard, encouraging more women to earn additional income to support the family as well. The unique culture of Thai society still establishes specific guidelines for women's career prospects. For instance, most employers in blue collar careers still prefer unmarried women, as they perceive married women as less committed to their jobs due to the expectation of women putting responsibilities toward family and household over job responsibilities. (Jitkaew & Omphornuwat 2019)

Nevertheless, traditional gender roles continue to have a significant impact on Thai society and culture. Understanding gender dynamics is crucial for navigating Thai relationships and fostering mutual respect and understanding between partners.

Protocols and Techniques for Communication

In Thai culture, non-confrontational and indirect communication styles are common, and respect and politeness are highly valued. These cultural values are reflected in common speech patterns and manners, with some customs intended to promote harmony and prevent conflict. (Malikhao, 2017)

One of the main characteristics of Thai communication is the use of the traditional greeting, "wai." The wai is a gesture of modest bowing and pressing one's palms together similar to how one prays. Saying hello, being respectful, and expressing gratitude to others are customs. A smile and a small head nod are usually given along with the wai. (Punjaroje & Morrison, 2007).

The concept of "greng jai," or maintaining one's dignity, is another essential facet of proper Thai communication. The secret to saving face is to refrain from doing anything that could embarrass oneself or others or make them feel less deserving of respect. This usually means staying out of direct conflict, criticism, or altercations in public places. Thais, on the other hand, may use subtle cues, nonverbal clues, and soft language to communicate harmoniously and avoid conflict. (Moussa, Doumani, McMurray, Muenjohn, & Deng, 2022)

When speaking Thai, it is important to be polite and respectful of others. This can include speaking to seniors or other people in positions of authority using titles and formal language. Even in informal situations, it is also usual to show others respect and gratitude.

In general, Thai people communicate in harmony, deference, and politeness. Understanding and following these cultural norms and etiquette can help people navigate social situations and show consideration for the feelings and sensitivities of others.

Because miscommunications can happen when Western communication styles collide with Thai customs, we'll offer advice on how to communicate effectively across cultural boundaries in relationships.

Marriage and Dating Customs

Thai dating customs can differ greatly from Western dating customs because they often reflect traditional values and cultural norms. In Thai culture, marriage is usually seen as involving family participation and following a variety of inherited traditions and customs.

One common dating custom in Thai culture is 'sin sod,' which refers to the bride's price or dowry that the groom pays to the bride's family. (Somswasdi, 2003) The Women's Movement and Legal Reform in Thailand. According to the tradition of 'sin sod,' it represents their appreciation and respect for raising and caring for their daughter. The concept of 'sin sod' has changed over time and is consistently important in many Thai communities, particularly in rural areas, even though it may not be highly valued in urban areas.

The "thong mun," or formal engagement ceremony, is an important part of Thai dating culture. At Thong Mun, a formal event where the groom asks the bride for her hand in marriage in front of her family and close relatives, the bride accepts. This ceremony may include official engagement papers being signed, blessings from elders, and gift-giving.

In addition to these customs, Thai dating usually involves close involvement and approval from family members, especially parents. The family is significant in Thai culture, and parents' opinions and approval are highly considered when it comes to marriage and relationships. As such, couples may seek the consent and advice of their families before making important relationship decisions. (Kepner, 2023)

In summary, Thai dating customs are deeply related to cultural belief and tradition, giving the importance of family relationships, respect to elders, and submission to rituals and customs. Many of these traditions are still important in Thai society, even though modernization and globalization have had an influence on some aspects of Thai dating culture.

Western men who are interested in dating Thai women should be aware of these customs and approach dating with consideration for this cultural aspect.

Including Thai Customs and Values in the Partnership

By accepting Thai traditions and beliefs, you could improve your bond with your partner and help them get to know you better. Here are a few ways you and your partner can appreciate Thai culture:

1. Appreciating Older People

Older people are respected greatly in Thai society. When making important decisions, seek insight and recommendations from your partner's parents and other elders. Always treat them with kindness and modesty.

2. Commitment and Loyalty

These two qualities are very important in Thai relationships. Your loyalty to your partner and the relationship will be shown by making their needs a priority, encouraging them when they go through difficult times, and being trustworthy and attentive.

3. Family Values

Thai society places a high value on family. Make an effort to get connected with your partner's family and let them know how much you respect and admire their familial ties. To strengthen your relationships with your loved ones, take part in activities that bring you together.

4. Modesty and Humility

In Thai culture, these are two of the most admired characteristics. Create a sense of modesty and sincerity whenever you communicate with other people. Instead, show humility. Keep a mindset of thankfulness and appreciate the little things in life.

5. The teachings of Buddhism

Buddhism, the official religion of Thailand, has a profound effect on Thai society and culture. Integrate Buddhist principles such as compassion, mindfulness, and kindness into your relationship. Show your lover and everyone else how much you care by being kind and patient.

6. Avoiding Conflict and Building Harmony

Maintaining peace and avoiding quarrels are highly regarded in Thai culture. Seek peaceful compromises by respectfully confronting disagreements of viewpoint. Learning to listen attentively and being flexible may do miracles for your relationship.

7. Religion, Myths, and Superstitions

Spirituality and superstitions exist in Thai society. Be tolerant of your partner's customs and faith while taking part in their ceremonies and rituals without judgment. Pay respect to sacred places and ceremonies.

8. Hospitality and Generosity

In Thai culture, extending hospitality and generosity is highly valued. Show kindness to your partner and others, and give guests a hearty welcome. When guests come over to your house, share meals with them and extend a warm welcome.

9. Celebrations & Festivities

Thai traditions and customs are shown clearly and vigorously through festivals and celebrations. Join in the holiday spirit of the season by engaging with celebrations of major Thai festivals, including Songkran (the New Year) and Loy Krathong (the Festival of Lights).

10. Cultural Sensitivity and Adaptability

Be respectful, sensitive, and inquisitive while engaging with Thai culture. Learn to understand the regulations, rules, and practices of Thai culture. The next stage is to be flexible and embrace these subtle cultural differences in your relationship. Let yourself become fascinated by the beauty and variation in Thai culture. Respect, understanding, and admiration for one another's cultural background may be developed in a relationship by accepting Thai values and practices. Embrace the rich variety of Thailand, and let it deepen your relationship as a couple.

Recognizing the Significance of Community and Family in Thai Culture

In Thai culture, one's family and community have a major effect on shaping one's identity and beliefs. One way to better understand Thai relationships and culture is to learn about the value of family and community. Some important considerations are as follows:

1. Building a Foundation

For Thais, the family is the fundamental social structure. In Thai houses which date back many generations, people usually maintain secure relationships with both their immediate and extended family.

2. Respect and Commitment to Family

Respect one's parents and other seniors is highly valued in Thai society, a practice known as filial piety. Taking good care of one's parents, grandparents, and other older people is a crucial life skill for children to learn. In order to maintain harmony in the family, it is believed that expressing appreciation and respect to the elders is important.

3. Collective Responsibility

Thai culture strongly emphasizes mutual support and collective responsibility within communities. Gatherings of friends, acquaintances, and neighbors are common occasions for holiday celebrations, mutual assistance, and group activities. Strong feelings of harmony and belonging are fostered by such unity.

4. Support Systems

Thais rely on their social networks for both emotional and practical support. Close-knit communities provide safety protection in difficult times by providing childcare, financial assistance, and other services. Building and sustaining supportive relationships is highly valued in Thai culture.

5. The Role of Leaders and Elders

In Thai societies, respected elders and authority figures include parents, grandparents, teachers, and religious leaders. They are highly regarded for their expertise and advice, which is regularly sought in matters concerning family, education, and personal development.

6. Customs and Traditions within the Family

Several traditions and customs performed by Thai families reinforce their connections to their ancestors and to one another. Weddings, baby showers, and religious rituals are all great opportunities for families to get together, become closer, and share traditions from a generation to the next.

7. Relationships Across Generations

Grandparents take an active role in their grandchildren's upbringing, since Thai culture places a great importance on intergenerational relationships. One way that people of different ages might stay connected is through the practice of passing on wisdom, values, and traditions from one generation to the next.

8. Strong Sense of Duty and Obligation

There is a deep feeling of responsibility to one's family and community among Thai people. It is believed that it is essential to maintain social standards, take care of family responsibilities, and work to better the lives of others. It is believed that the morals of giving and caring should be upheld.

9. Community Spirituality

A few examples of the spiritual practices and beliefs that Thai communities commonly share are merit-making ceremonies, Buddhist rituals, and temple visits. Through the promotion of a sense of shared identity and communal spirituality, these group activities strengthen bonds of unity and interdependence.

10. Preserving Customs and Legacy

Maintaining and transferring cultural customs and legacies to future generations depends on Thai families. Stories, rituals, food, and traditions all play a role in the passing down of Thai culture and language from one generation to the next.

People will have a greater awareness of the values that guide Thai society and the interdependence of all relationships when they learn about the importance of family and community in Thai culture. In order to maintain harmony, Thai communities must respect cultural traditions, promote a sense of belonging, and protect relationships between families.

Ways to Overcome Cultural Differences and Other Obstacles in Relationships

Overcoming cultural differences in a relationship with a Thai partner might be challenging, but it's possible to do so with patience, understanding, and effective communication. Here are some ways you and your Thai partner could move beyond cultural barriers and other relationship challenges:

Have a deeper appreciation for your Thai partner's background and perspective by familiarizing yourself with their culture, traditions, and customs. You must keep in mind that they may not share your values, beliefs, or standard of living.

1. Encourage Frank and Open Conversation

To prevent or settle any cultural misunderstandings, ask your Thai partner to talk openly and honestly with you. The environment of mutual understanding and respect enables people to talk about their views on culture, boundaries, and standards.

2. Being Adaptable and Patient

Be adaptable and patient, and keep in mind that people from other cultures may have different expectations of you. You should have an open mind and be prepared to compromise when dealing with situations, although cultural differences may frequently trigger misunderstandings or confrontations.

3. Working Together for a Common Goal

Discover a solution to relationship issues or cultural differences that works for everyone by working together and compromising. To resolve disagreements, you must find a middle ground that takes into account the cultural norms and beliefs of both parties.

4. Appreciation of Personal Varieties

Appreciate the unique qualities that make you and your Thai partner unique, and know that the variety in your relationship is a strength. Instead of trying to force your cultural beliefs and standards on your partner, embrace cultural differences as a chance to learn and develop.

5. Ask for Help and Guidance

Consult loved ones or cultural advisers for assistance in understanding and negotiating cross-cultural interactions. obtain involved with intercultural couples' online forums or support groups to talk about your struggles, obtain advice, and learn strategies for overcoming cultural obstacles.

6. Cultivate Awareness and Compassion

Remember that your Thai partner may have had different experiences and come from a different cultural background than your own, and make an effort to understand and empathize with them. Building bridges between cultures and fostering mutual respect and understanding requires skills like active listening, empathy, and compassion.

7. Welcome and Celebrate Differences

Create an environment where each partner feels loved and accepted just the way they are by accepting diversity and inclusiveness in your relationship. In your interactions with your Thai partner, make an effort to celebrate different cultures and develop mutual acceptance and understanding.

8. Pay Attention to Common Aims and Values

You may build a strong foundation for your relationship and mutual respect by focusing on similar values, ambitions, and objectives that go beyond cultural differences. Love, trust, and compatibility should serve as the foundations of your foundation. The next step is to work together to achieve shared goals, which will strengthen your bond.

You and your Thai partner may overcome relationship challenges and cultural stereotypes with these strategies. Together, you can build a healthy and lasting partnership built on love, respect, and understanding. Building a satisfying relationship that honors each partner's tradition and beliefs requires patience and effort to overcome cultural gaps.

MYTH-BUSTING 2 THAI WOMEN ARE ALL THE SAME:

EXPLORING DIVERSITY AND INDIVIDUALITY

Acknowledging the Variations Among Thai Women

Many diverse cultures coexist in Thailand, and as a result, local languages, traditions, and customs vary greatly throughout the country. From the peaceful countryside to the chaotic city of Bangkok, Thai ladies come from all walks of life. Moreover, ethnic diversity plays a role; Thais come from a wide variety of ethnic origins, including Chinese, Thai, and other groups, all of which contribute to the country's rich cultural tapestry.

Comprehending Socioeconomic Considerations

The upbringing, values, and objectives of a person are significantly influenced by their socioeconomic class. It is possible that rural Thai women and urban Thai women have different perspectives on life and ways of living. Factors such as educational attainment, job aspirations, and financial stability explain why Thai women's experiences vary.

Embracing Diversity

The women of Thailand, like the women of every other country, are unique individuals with their own specific histories, cultures, and ways of life. Different individuals have different personalities; some may be shy and quiet, while others could be rather outspoken and confident. It is important to treat each Thai lady with the respect she deserves and not make assumptions about her based on generalizations or stereotypes.

Embracing Diversity in Dating

Discovering the diversity of Thai women can open up new opportunities for meaningful dialogue and relationships. Men from other countries are capable of creating stronger bonds and fostering understanding amongst women by respecting and valuing the unique experiences and backgrounds of each individual woman. Dating becomes more fun and leads to a more fulfilling relationship journey when diversity is acknowledged.

In conclusion, recognizing the diversity of Thai women is crucial for building healthy relationships and advancing a better understanding of Thai culture. With an embrace of Thai culture's distinctiveness and depth, foreign men can successfully navigate Thailand's dating scene with confidence, respect, and genuine interest.

Acknowledging Uniqueness and Distinctive Features

Honoring Individuality Diversity

Thai women, like women from every country, display a wide range of characteristics and personality traits. Someone may be more introverted and reserved, whereas another may be more extroverted and sociable. Personality and mindset in life are shaped by a woman's unique combination of values, beliefs, and interests.

Acknowledging Cultural Influences

Social norms and cultural upbringing have a big impact on Thai women's personalities. They might be deeply ingrained with a strong sense of humility, respect for elders, and loyalty to their family. Travel, education, and modern influences from foreign media all contribute to Thai women's diverse personalities.

Reflecting on Past Experiences

The people a woman knows, the job she did in the past, and her degree of education all shape her character. Thai women's life experiences might differ considerably according to their geography, social level, and family history. In addition to shaping their character and behavior, these circumstances also influence their expectations, ambitions, and perspectives.

Understanding Your Areas of Strength and Growth

As a result of her individuality, every woman has her own set of opportunities and difficulties. Although some individuals are very ambitious and driven, others put an emphasis on their personal relationships and families. A more meaningful connection and mutual respect may develop in relationships when people take the time to understand and value one another's unique qualities.

Celebrating Individuality

Dating Thai women is more enjoyable when you accept and embrace their unique characteristics. Males from outside Thailand would do well to avoid generalizations about Thai women and instead respect their distinctive character and individuality. Foreign men can build healthy relationships with women based on mutual understanding and respect by recognizing the individuality of each woman.

In conclusion, accepting Thai women for who they are and their unique personalities is essential to building genuine and healthy relationships with them. By recognizing the diversity of Thai women's characteristics, experiences, and viewpoints, foreign men can build more deep relationships and meaningful bonds with them that are based on respect, understanding, and appreciation.

MYTH-BUSTING 3 HIGH-VALUE THAI WOMEN ARE UNATTAINABLE:

STRATEGIES FOR ATTRACTION AND CONNECTION

Knowing What Raises the Value of a Thai Woman

Cultural Customs and Values

High-value Thai women often embody traditional values such as respect, loyalty, and a strong emphasis on family. They may respect traditions and customs while also embracing modernity and tolerance. Their characters have greater depth and complexity because of their strong sense of cultural identity and ancestry.

Education and Intelligence

Many highly valued Thai women place a high emphasis on education and mental growth. They may seek advanced degrees, work toward professional careers, or always be learning new things. Their intelligence, curiosity, and critical thinking skills make them fascinating conversationalists and interesting company.

Motivation and Aspiration

There are a lot of respected Thai women who have high expectations for themselves and always want to achieve their best. Their relationships, careers, and personal endeavors are marked by unwavering determination, resilience, and a constant dedication to achievement.

Kindness and Understanding

Kindness, empathy, and compassion are traits shown by highly valued Thai women. They provide understanding, support, and encouragement to others around them because they are emotionally intelligent and perceptive. Strong emotional bonds and positive connections grow under their caring character.

High standard Thai women are recognized for their independence, self-sufficiency, and autonomy.

They are independent, capable, and brave; they make their own decisions and take responsibility for their shortcomings. Their self-assurance and independence add to their attractiveness and charm.

Cultural Flexibility and Open-Mindedness

A large number of highly valued Thai women are accepting of various cultures and flexible in their thinking. They are excited and curious about variety, new experiences, and opposing points of view. Their curiosity and willingness to interact with the outside world improve their lives and relationships.

In conclusion, understanding what makes a Thai woman highly valued requires realizing and appreciating a combination of cultural values, personal characteristics, and life experiences. When foreign men recognize and value these qualities in Thai women, they can build deeper and more meaningful relationships with them.

Useful Advice for Reaching and Establishing Relationships with High-Value Thai Women

Respect Thai culture and customs

Learn about social mores, manners, and customs in order to acknowledge and honor Thai traditions and customs. Express genuine interest in and admiration for Thai cuisine, language, and culture. Engage in cultural events and activities together to improve understanding and your relationship.

Display Your Sincerity and Confidence

When engaging with Thai women, project a genuine, self- assured, and authentic personality. Refrain from being fake or overly dramatic; instead, be authentic, honest, and true to who you are. Maintaining reasonable boundaries and self- assurance shows that you respect both other people and yourself.

Be Respectful and Effective in Your Communication

Show empathy, understanding, and active listening when interacting with Thai women. Take note of cultural quirks and nonverbal clues, and adjust your communication style accordingly. Encourage frank and insightful conversation, communicate in a direct, honest, and polite manner.

Show Ambition and Drive

If you want to attract Thai women, you should show them that you are ambitious, determined, and committed by displaying your successes and goals. Always put in your best effort and show that you have a strong work ethic. Gain respect and recognition for your determination and passion for self-improvement.

Display Your Curiosity and Intelligence

Encourage thought-provoking dialogues and exchanges that highlight your knowledge, curiosity, and intelligence. Start a conversation that will make Thai women ponder by telling them about yourself, your interests, and your skills. Display your ability for logical thinking, creative thinking, and problem-solving in a variety of situations.

Develop Emotional Bonding and Complementarity

When it comes to developing chemistry and an emotional bond with Thai women, sincere warmth, affection, and empathy are essential.

Build rapport, intimacy, and trust by sharing personal experiences, feelings, and experiences.

Create memorable moments and exchanges with others that will strengthen your bond.

Respect individuality and freedom

respecting Thai women's freedom, show them respect for their independence, autonomy, and self-reliance.

Refrain from being controlling or possessive, so Thai women can continue to be unique and follow their passions.

Encourage and assist them in achieving their individual goals and aspirations in order to see success.

In conclusion, by following this practical advice for attracting and connecting with high-value Thai women, foreign men can successfully cope with the dating circumstances with confidence, authenticity, and respect. Men who value personal development, effective communication, and cultural sensitivity can establish enduring relationships with Thai women who respect their qualities and values.

MYTH-BUSTING 4 THAI WOMEN ARE ONLY INTERESTED IN WEALTH:

DISPELLING MATERIALISTIC STEREOTYPES

Thai women are influenced by a wide range of goals and dreams that go beyond just making money. The pursuit of one's own interests, goals, and passions is a powerful motivator for many Thai women. Since they find fulfillment in growing one's career and one's personal life, they actively seek out partnerships that will help them do just that.

The importance of connection and companionship in romantic relationships is highly valued by Thai women, and this can be a strong motivator for them. People in this situation look for people who can relate to them and provide them with emotional support. By encouraging the development of deep connections and cherished experiences, friendship increases a feeling of connection and belonging.

A strong emotional bond is valued by Thai women because they think the most fulfilling relationships are those that are built on trust, respect, and love. They look for companions who are capable of developing strong emotional bonds, communicating openly, and expressing understanding.

Intimacy and a strong basis can be created by an emotional connection between partners.

The many and complicated reasons behind Thai women's actions reflect their own values, objectives, and aspirations in their personal and professional lives. Seeking opportunities for emotional happiness relationships, and personal development, they seek out deep relationships that go beyond stereotypes and show the wide range of their experiences and ambitions.

MYTH-BUSTING 5 DATING THAI GIRLS IS ONLY FOR CASUAL FUN:

EMBRACING THE POTENTIAL FOR DEEP CONNECTION

Busting Preconceived Notions about Casual Dating

Dating Thai women is often associated with preconceived notions that they are primarily interested in casual relationships or materialistic pursuits. These misconceptions state that Thai women are only attracted to foreigners for casual or romantic relationships. However, it's important to recognize that Thai women have diverse backgrounds and goals in life.

Like women from any other culture, many Thai women are looking for deep connections and long-term commitment. In a relationship, they value company, emotional connection, and shared experiences. Prioritizing material comfort or financial security may be important to some Thai women, but compatibility, emotional closeness, and personal fulfillment are valued by others.

Examining Emotional Depth and Connection

As with relationships with partners from any culture, developing healthy relationships with Thai women requires strong emotional intimacy and connection. These elements of a relationship delve into the depths of understanding, trust, and vulnerability and go beyond simple physical attraction or common interests. Being emotionally connected with a Thai woman requires you to be open and honest. Open and honest communication between couples strengthens mutual understanding and empathy by allowing them to openly express their needs, emotions, and opinions. Being a patient and attentive listener who pays close attention to both verbal and nonverbal cues is essential in Thai culture, which places importance on indirect communication and avoiding confrontation.

Another essential component of emotional intimacy in partnerships with Thai women is trust. It takes time, consistency, dependability, and integrity in both words and actions to establish trust. A sense of emotional intimacy and connection is built on trust, which makes partners feel safe and supported.

Being vulnerable is crucial to strengthening your emotional connections with Thai women. Being open about one's worries, insecurities, and goals without worrying about criticism or rejection is what it means to be vulnerable. A deep feeling of intimacy and connection develops from giving to one's partner's complete acceptance and understanding of oneself.

Being patient, compassionate, and truly involved in your partner's personal life are key elements for developing a close relationship and connection. It involves being mindful, responding with compassion and understanding, and paying close attention. Couples who prioritize communication, trust, and vulnerability can build their emotional connection and foster understanding. You can use this to lay the foundation for a healthy relationship with Thai women.

Managing Relationship Expectations

A study of Thai women's typical expectations and desires in relationships indicates that stability, security, and emotional support rank highly. Thai women frequently look for a partner who can give them a sense of stability and security in both their financial and emotional lives. Relationships founded on trust, honest communication, and mutual respect are respected by them since they allow them to feel supported and valued in such relationships. Foreign guys interested in dating Thai women should align their expectations and seek to have a healthy relationship. Foreign men can deal with relationship dynamics more skillfully if they comprehend and respect Thai culture's emphasis on security and stability.

Here are some tips for matching expectations and aspirations in a relationship with Thai women:

Talk Honestly

Communicating clearly and openly from the start enables both partners to freely express their needs, wants, and expectations. To ensure mutual understanding, encourage open communication about priorities, long-term plans, and relationship goals.

Put Emotional Support First

In relationships, Thai women place a high importance on emotional support and connection. Be willing to listen to your partner's thoughts and feelings and to demonstrate empathy and understanding. When things are tough, reassure and support your partner emotionally to demonstrate your commitment to them.

Exhibit Dependability and Consistency

In Thai culture, these qualities are highly valued. Show that you are dependable by keeping your word and acting consistently throughout your behavior. This strengthens the relationship's foundation of confidence and trust.

Respect Cultural Differences

To build a strong relationship with Thai women, one must honor Thai traditions and culture. Respect Thai cultural heritage by spending some time learning about their customs, values, and beliefs. Accept cultural differences as learning and development opportunities rather than as barriers.

Be Understanding and Patient

It takes time and patience to establish a harmonious relationship. As you work through cultural differences and modify your expectations of one another, have patience with your partner. To create a relationship that works for both of you, be flexible, understanding, and willing to give in when necessary. Foreign men can develop healthy relationships with Thai women that are built on mutual respect, understanding, and love by learning about common relationship expectations.

Foreign men can create loving, mutually respectful, and fulfilling partnerships with Thai women by learning about common relationship expectations and desires among Thai women and talking about ways to align relationship goals and expectations.

Establishing Trust and Commitment

Establishing solid foundations for healthy relationships with Thai women requires a great deal of trust, honesty, and integrity. These characteristics, which promote emotional stability, understanding, and respect for one another, serve as the foundation of a fulfilling relationship.

Because they give a relationship a sense of security and comfort, Thai women cherish relationships based on honesty and trust. Being sincere and honest in word and action are necessary for building credibility. Never intentionally mislead or hide information from your partner; always be open about your objectives, feelings, and expectations.

Another crucial component in building mutual respect and trust in a partnership is integrity. Remaining strong in your opinions and values, no matter what it takes, will show your partner that you are dependable and trustworthy. When communicating with one another, making decisions, and handling conflicts, it is critical to do it in a respectful way.

Consistent communication, respecting boundaries, and sharing experiences are practical ways to show Thai women that you are dependable and committed to them. Regular, honest conversation in which you both feel comfortable sharing your feelings, ideas, and worries is a key component of consistent communication with your partner. Maintain open ways of communication and try to actively and sympathetically hear what your partner has to say.

Respecting one another's boundaries is a crucial component of maintaining partnerships that are strong and trusted. Your partner has a right to their personal time, privacy, and emotional well-being, and you should respect them. Never put your partner in a situation where they feel insecure; doing so can only result in mistrust and a breakdown in communication. On the contrary, while negotiating boundaries in conversation, be open and truthful.

Your relationship with your partner may be strengthened through shared experiences, which build lasting memories and deepen your bond. Whether you're going on journeys, doing things you both love, or just hanging out and relaxing, appreciate the time you spend doing these things together. A feeling of togetherness can grow in a relationship when everyone involved shares experiences and makes memories with one another.

Relationships with Thai women that last for a long time depend on three things: honesty, integrity, and respect. You can build a strong and meaningful relationship by placing a value on trust, respect, and love for one another, and by actively showing commitment and reliability via actions like sharing stories, being in frequent communication, and respecting boundaries.

Finally, if you want to have a healthy, happy relationship with a Thai woman, you need to work on building mutual growth and support. By prioritizing each other's goals, sharing in each other's achievements, and working through conflicts with respect and understanding, you can build an honest and fulfilling relationship that enables both partners to grow and achieve in every aspect of their lives.

MYTH-BUSTING 6 THAI WOMEN ARE SUBMISSIVE:

CELEBRATING STRENGTH, INDEPENDENCE, AND EMPOWERMENT

Diversity is Strength

Thai women have been shaped into what they are now by their many interesting and diverse life experiences. The determination and fortitude that characterize each individual's history are often made open in such interactions. Many factors, including individual experiences, family relationships, and cultural customs, influence Thai women's resilience.

The deeply embedded values and customs of Thai society have a major effect on the resilience of Thai women. From an early age, Thai women learn the importance of being strong, flexible, and peacemakers in their families and communities. Cultural values in Thailand encourage strength and perseverance, which helps Thai women face adversity with grace and calm.

Family dynamics are another important factor that shapes Thai women's resilience. Thai families are very close-knit and offer a strong sense of belonging and support. Women are stronger than adversity when they have this foundation of love and security. Thai women gain valuable life skills, guidance and support, and the strength to confront obstacles in the family.

The personal experiences of Thai women, which empower them to face life's difficulties directly, are an additional proof of their strength and courage. Whether it's because of expectations from society, personal struggles, or financial limitations, Thai women always find a way to overcome these obstacles and pursue their goals.

It is clear that they are resilient because of their ability to adapt to new circumstances, overcome challenges, and rise even stronger than before.

Finally, cultural factors, relationships with family members, and individual experiences all play a role in shaping Thai women's resilience. Thai women show amazing strength as they face and overcome many challenges in life. Their various histories, experiences, and journeys all add to stories that demonstrate the power that characterizes every person's own journey.

Managing Social Expectations

Thai women face social pressures mostly caused by cultural norms, traditional gender roles, and family responsibilities. Responsibilities like caring for others, maintaining harmony in the home, and prioritizing family above personal objectives may be part of these expectations. Yet, an increasing number of Thai women are standing up to these stereotypes and asserting their independence to follow career paths of their own.

The traditional role of women in Thai culture is to stay at home and raise children, while men are expected to work outside the house to provide for their families. In opposition to these expectations, an increasing number of Thai women are going to university, working full-time, and fighting for financial independence. When more Thai women break down barriers and pursue careers in traditionally male-dominated sectors like business, politics, and STEM (science, technology, engineering, and mathematics), we will see a shift in society's views on gender roles and stereotypes.

Family responsibilities also play a major part in shaping the social expectations of Thai women. Keeping order at home and supporting the needs of one's family are concepts taught to young Thai women. Thai women are finding ways to balance their individual goals with their family responsibilities, despite the cultural focus on family. Among these duties may include communicating what they want and need, setting boundaries, and resolving conflicts with relatives.

Societal norms around family life and marriage could influence the expectations put on women in Thailand. Many Thai women choose to delay marriage or stay single so they can focus on their careers and personal growth, even though getting married and establishing a family are seen as important life milestones. Additionally, more and more people are accepting and encouraging women who want to be single parents. This is leading to a change in how society views single parenting.

In spite of every aspect, Thai women are showing their independence, pursuing their dreams, and negotiating and confronting societal conventions. The battle for gender equality, social transformation, and empowerment is being fought by Thai women via education, activism, and advocacy. Transforming society and motivating the next generation, Thai women are breaking norms and making their own paths.

Overcoming Adversity

Even when things get difficult, Thai women are determined and creative; they also work hard to make a better life for their families. Regardless of social norms or other barriers, Thai women are courageous and do not give up on their goals. Adversity doesn't discourage them; they gracefully handle complex social dynamics, financial constraints, and cultural standards. No matter the challenge, Thai women are fearless and determined. whether it's in the pursuit of higher education, starting a company, or their struggle for equal rights.

In addition, Thai women are very creative when it comes to figuring out how to accomplish their objectives, even when faced with challenges. To get through in a world where opportunities are few, they rely on their social networks, innovative thinking, and adaptability. Thai women are always finding new ways to put their creative energies to good use, whether it's through donating or starting their own small businesses.

DO & DON'T OF APPROACHING THAI GIRLS

Dos and Don'ts of Approaching Thai Girls

In order to build strong connections and relationships with Thai girls, it is important that you treat them with respect. The things that you should and should not do are as follows:

Dos:

1. Show Respect

Approach Thai girls with respect and genuine interest. Show appreciation for their culture, traditions, and values.

2. Be Polite

If you want to attract a Thai girl, you need to communicate with her politely. The polite things to say are "sawasdee kab" (hello) and "khob khun kab" (thank you).

3. Learn Some Thai

Learning basic Thai phrases can show your effort and interest in their culture. Practice simple greetings and expressions.

4. Be Patient

Initially, Thai girls could be more reserved and shy. Wait for them to get comfortable around you; it will take time.

5. Engage in Active Listening

Listen attentively while communicating with Thai girls. Show that you are interested in what they are saying and that you care about what they say by asking them questions.

6. Respect Your Personal Space

Remain mindful of your personal space and refrain from being unduly pushy or intruding.

7. Express Sincere Interest in Their Culture

Be genuinely curious about Thai customs, cuisine, holidays, and culture. This indicates that you value and respect their history.

8. Give Thoughtful Compliments

When praising someone, be sincere, but avoid being overly personal or confrontational. Take note of qualities such as intelligence, kindness, or inventiveness.

9. Be Honest

When engaging with Thai girls, be truthful and open about your intentions. Stay away from lying or playing games.

10. Recognize Cultural Norms

Learn the basics of Thai culture, which includes things like removing shoes before entering a house, not showing love in public, and respecting the elderly.

Avoid:

1. Form Presumptions

Refrain from drawing conclusions about Thai girls based on generalizations or stereotypes. Show respect to every person and evaluate them according to their behavior and character.

2. Pressuring Thai girls to Make Decisions Right Away

Refrain from pressuring them to make decisions right away. Recognize and honor their need for time to reflect and react.

3. Disrespect Cultural Customs

Steer clear of disregarding or belittling Thai traditions or customs. Be mindful of traditions such as Buddhism, honor the monarchy, and show deference to elders.

4. Use Offensive Language

Refrain from disparaging Thai culture, people, or customs with offensive language.

5. Act Aggressively

When interacting with Thai girls, refrain from acting aggressively or confrontationally. Retain a composed and courteous manner.

6. Assume Homogeneity

Be sensitive to the idea that people's life experiences, upbringings, and cultural backgrounds can significantly influence Thai lifestyles. Keep in mind that not everyone in Thailand is the same.

7. Be Overly Forward

Refrain from approaching people inappropriately or in an overly forward manner. Be mindful of boundaries and proceed with caution.

8. Ignore Consent

When interacting with Thai girls, always give consent priority. Be mindful of their personal space and avoid doing anything that could cause them to feel unsafe or uneasy.

9. Neglect Personal Hygiene

Keep your personal cleaning and grooming in mind. Good grooming is a sign of self-respect and social-respect.

10. Hasty Relationship Development

Don't rush into getting romantically involved with a Thai girl. Take your time building a trustworthy relationship, and be mindful of their speed.

By following these dos and don'ts, you can approach Thai girls in a polite manner and establish relationships based on respect and understanding.

SUSTAINING PASSION AND A HEALTHY RELATIONSHIP WITH A THAI GIRL

Maintaining a Healthy Romantic Relationship with a Thai Girl

Keeping the spark alive in the relationship is important to keep the love and vitality of the two of you healthy and thriving. If you want your romance with a Thai girl to remain passionate, take these steps:

1. Show How Much You Care Frequently.

Your Thai lover will appreciate it if you show them how much you care about them frequently. Show her how much you care by cuddling her and showing your appreciation for everything that she does.

2. Plan Unexpected Dates and Vacations

Surprise your partner with dates or trips to keep the romance alive. A romantic evening at her favorite restaurant or a weekend trip to a beautiful place are two examples of surprising presents that may ignite passion in your relationship.

3. Discover Thai Culture Together

As a way of educating yourself in your partner's culture, learn about Thai festivals, customs, and food. To show that you care about her ethnic background while building a more intimate connection with her, try cooking Thai food together at home, participating in festivals, or learning some basic Thai words.

4. Maintain Open and Honest Communication

Open and honest communication is key to having a healthy relationship. Listen carefully to what your Thai partner has to say and be honest with her about your feelings, objectives, and thoughts. Express empathy and respect for her viewpoints.

5. **Make an Effort to Understand What She Enjoys Doing**

Show an interest in your partner's passions, interests, and hobbies. In order to deepen your bond with her, you should do things like encourage her to follow her passions.

6. **Create Treasured Memories**

To build memories that last, make an effort to allocate time together doing exciting things and discovering more about the world. Whether you're traveling the world, trying out new activities, or just chilling at home, enjoy every moment you spend with your partner and make memories that will last a lifetime.

7. **Take Thoughtful Actions to Surprise Her**

Not expected, thoughtful acts are an excellent way to show your Thai partner how much you care. Trying something as simple as bringing her her favorite flowers, cooking her favorite meal, or writing a heartfelt note may have a profound effect on your relationship.

8. **Keep the Passion in Your Bedroom**

Keep passion alive in bed if you want your love life to be exciting. Be bold and thoughtful when it comes to relationships and intimacy if you want to keep the spark alive in your relationship.

9. **Acknowledge Important Moments and Celebrate Achievements**

Try to mark your calendars for all the important dates, including anniversaries in your relationship, birthdays, anniversaries, and holidays. Plan romantic surprises, exchange nice presents, and create memorable experiences that nurture your love.

10. Prioritize Quality Time Together

Regardless of how busy your schedules are, you should always make time to spend with each other. Whether it's on a romantic walk or a cozy evening in front of the TV, spending quality time together without distractions benefits relationships and keeps passion alive.

If you and your Thai partner want to keep the romance and grow stronger as a couple, consider trying out some of this advice. Never forget to prioritize communication, show appreciation, and keep your relationship as passionate and loving as ever.

Innovative Date Ideas and Activities to Keep the Spark

If you want to keep the romance alive and grow it with your Thai partner, here are some great date ideas and things to do to create memories that will last a lifetime with your partner:

1. A Class on Thai Cooking

Taking a Thai cooking class is a great way to learn the secrets and techniques of making original and delicious Thai food. As you both prepare and taste delicious Thai foods, you'll strengthen the relationship through shared enthusiasm for this food.

2. Go to Local Markets

Enjoy and visit street food stalls and local markets to try genuine Thai food and amazing items. Visiting the lively atmosphere of Thailand's busy markets is a must.

3. Beach Picnic

Bring all of those favorite sweets, drinks, and snacks for a lovely beach picnic. Get some sunlight, swim in the water, and spend the day relaxing on the beach with your partner.

4. Cultural Exploration

Explore the fascinating history of Thailand by taking an informal tour of historic places, galleries, and temples. Get yourself into Thai history, art, and the country's cultural sites.

5. Trips to Nature

Experience the beautiful environment by going kayaking, hiking, or riding through some of Thailand's gorgeous national parks. Get together to see the amazing scenery of Thailand and immerse yourself in nature while having exciting excursions.

6. A Day in a Spa

Relax yourself with an hour at the spa, filled with soothing massages and other therapies. Charge your batteries while spending precious time together in a relaxing spa ambience.

7. Sailing at Sunset

Experience a romantic sunset sailing along one of Thailand's beautiful rivers. Spend quality time with your partner while enjoying the beautiful evening vibe.

8. Cultural Performances

Check out concerts featuring traditional Thai music, puppetry, and dance performances. Experience Thailand's dynamic cultural landscape and be fascinated by the grace and skill of its performing arts.

9. Volunteer Together

As a group, volunteer in your community for a worthwhile cause or charitable organization. Enhance the lives of others while building a strong relationship and common values as a couple.

10. Stargazing Night

Arrange a romantic evening in a remote area far from the lights of the city to watch the stars. Lay a blanket out beneath the stars, snuggle close, and enjoy the starry sky while talking about your hopes and dreams.

11. Doing Art and Activities Creatively

For better creativity between you and your partner, think about participating in creating classes or connecting with people who share your passion while fulfilling your passion through the creation of beautiful handmade products or artwork.

Taking trips, experiencing new things, and making unforgettable experiences together is a great way to keep the romance alive and build the connection with your Thai partner. These will make your relationship healthy and enjoyable.

A Growth of Connection and a Strong Emotional Connection

In order to have a healthy relationship with your Thai partner, it is important to build up feelings of intimacy. You may get more attached to each other and build the connection between you and your partner by using any of the following methods:

1. Support Honest and Open Conversation

Communicate openly and honestly with your partner about your thoughts, feelings, and situations in life. Allow your Thai partner to share their opinions and emotions and listen intently without judgement.

2. Listening With Intent

Listen attentively to your Thai partner, make eye contact, and show that you understand what they are saying. Validate their emotions to make them feel heard and important in the relationship.

3. Spending Time With One Another

Plan occasional date nights and other quality time together to strengthen your bond and emotional connection. Spend quality time with your partner by doing things like going out to dinner, watching Netflix, or even just spending time on the couch together.

4. Shared Hobbies and Interests

Meet up with your Thai partner for fun activities based on common passions or hobbies. You can deepen your relationship and create memories that will last for a long time if you do things together, such as traveling, sharing passionate activities, or just cooking or baking.

5. Showing Understanding and Compassion

When your Thai partner is going through a difficult time, be there for them, understanding, and supportive. Show that you care about their feelings and experiences while reminding her of your love.

6. Physical Love

Thai partners like shows of intimacy and love such as hugs, kisses, and cuddling. Because these actions can build emotional safety and warmth in a relationship, loving acts and expressions of love should be prioritized.

7. Appreciation and Respect

Thank your Thai partner for everything that they've done and the helpful acts that they've made to the relationship.

Expressing your appreciation and respect for their qualities and traits will make them feel valued and appreciated in the relationship.

8. Common Expectations and Goals

To develop shared goals and a shared future with your Thai partner, it's beneficial to share your aims, plans, and ambitions with them. Partner in setting objectives and planning to strengthen your relationship and build your emotional connection.

9. Trust and Being Vulnerable

To increase openness and trust in your relationship with your Thai partner, be open, honest, and vulnerable. Being vulnerable and open about your worries, stress, and weaknesses will make a safe space for her to do the same.

10. Patience and Understanding

Show patience and understanding in your relationships, particularly when overcoming communication obstacles and cultural differences. Approach conflicts and disagreements with empathy and understanding, and be patient with each other's flaws and differences.

An emotionally bonded relationship between you and your Thai partner might be built through standard, open conversations, spending quality time together, engaging in similar interests, and giving each other emotional support. If you want your relationship to go on, it's important to give attention to the growth of trust and understanding and to work on being vulnerable with your partner.

MARRIAGE LAW/VISA, LAWSUIT AGAINST ADULTERY, PROPERTY OWNERSHIP AS A FOREIGNER, AND RETIREMENT

Communicating honestly and openly about major life decisions, such as marriage, having a kid, and relocating, is important for developing a strong and healthy relationship with your Thai partner. You may check that your beliefs, goals, and expectations are compatible with one another through these talks as you plan for your future together. Talk about the following important subjects with your Thai partner:

1. Marriage

To begin, talk to your Thai partner about your thoughts on marriage and your plans for a future union. Discuss your expectations for a marriage or 'sinsord' tradition, what marriage means to you both, and any cultural or religious factors that might influence your choice. Be willing to talk about your ideal wedding date, your timeline for getting married, and your beliefs about getting engaged and getting married.

2. Family

Talk to your Thai partner about your expectations for creating or growing a family as well as your perspectives on family life. Talk about your goals for kids, parenting philosophies, and family dynamics. Also, make sure you're both at ease with your future roles and responsibilities. Be willing to talk about cultural customs, family traditions, and your plans for starting a family.

3. Relocation

Talk about your ideas about moving to a new place, either in Thailand or overseas, if relocation is an option in your relationship. Discuss your motivations for thinking about moving, such as professional prospects, educational goals, or personal preferences, and investigate the possible effects a move might have on your life, relationships, and future plans.

Openly discuss your expectations, fears, and worries regarding the move with others, and work together to find solutions for any problems or obstacles that might arise.

4. Cultural Differences

Talk about how your relationship and future plans may be impacted by any cultural differences you and your Thai partner may have. Acknowledge and embrace these differences. It is important to learn about and respect each other's culture and beliefs. Also, remember to listen to your partner to learn their points of view. Take advantage of these conversations to strengthen your relationship and your bond as a multicultural couple.

5. Communication and Compromise

Make sure there is open communication, respectful listening, and mutual respect during your talks about marriage, family, and moving. When resolving disagreements or differences that may arise, exercise patience and understanding, and be prepared to compromise and find common ground on significant issues. Recall that having good communication with your Thai partner is essential to developing a strong and peaceful relationship.

6. Future Planning

Talk about your long-term objectives, hopes, and dreams as a couple and take some time to picture your future together.

Discuss your future goals as a couple, the milestones you intend to reach, and the ways you will assist one another's personal development. Plan ahead for your future as a couple and make a commitment to collaborate as a team to realize your common goal.

7. Seeking Support

When discussing big issues with your Thai partner, don't be afraid to ask for assistance from trustworthy friends, family members, or relationship counselors if you run into problems or have any questions. To assist you in resolving complex issues with empathy and understanding, consider consulting a licensed professional therapist or mediator. Note that asking for support shows tenacity and attention to the long- term health of your relationship.

When you and your Thai partner have open and deep talks about marriage, families, and relocation, you can build the foundation for a healthy relationship based on understanding, respect, and trust. Take the initiative to raise important topics as a group. Aim to create a future where everyone can live in love, joy, and prosperity by approaching these discussions with empathy, honesty, and a shared desire.

Thailand's Marriage Registry

In Thailand, foreigners and Thai citizens can easily arrange and quickly complete a marriage. On a working day, between 8 a.m. and 3 p.m. you may sign the legal Thailand marriage registration at any district office in any province. In Thailand, you need to have original passports and proof that you are unmarried in order to marry a Thai woman. If your prior marriage ended in divorce or death, you need the original certificates. The Ministry of Foreign Affairs must receive a notarized official statement of non-attachment from your home embassy in Bangkok if you have never been married.

It's possible that your embassy will require proof of this.

It will cost 1,000 Thai Baht (US$30) for each legal statement required by the Thai authorities. Your home embassy in Bangkok will usually charge a fee for notarizing it, and the Thai Ministry of Foreign Affairs (MFA) charges a small fee for registering it and providing a certificate that permits you to marry legally anywhere in Thailand. The Thai marriage certificate must be officially translated into Thai following the ceremony; this will incur an additional cost.

Planning should be carefully thought out before getting married. The foreigner's property should be protected. It is suggested that you use the services of a Thai lawyer to draft a prenuptial agreement on your behalf. It is common in Thailand to include both Thai and English in prenuptial agreements. To make sure that the prenuptial agreement is legally effective and enforceable in both countries, it is crucial to keep in mind issues such as whether you can own assets in both countries. Thoroughly researching and signing prenuptial agreements lowers the possibility that you may be sued. (Siam Legal International, 2024a)

Also, it is recommended that you choose a Thai legal practice to assist you with the registration process for marriage in Thailand to avoid future legal problems.

Above all, a foreign partner who marries a Thai national does not automatically become the individual owner of a piece of land in this stunning tropical paradise. However, the laws about property ownership might change over time, keep yourself updated.

Lawsuit Against Adultery

According to Thai law, a spouse may file for divorce if they can demonstrate that their partner committed adultery. The innocent spouse may be entitled to a larger share of the marital assets or other benefits in the divorce settlement, as adultery is regarded as a fault-based basis for divorce.

Any third person involved in her husband's extramarital affair, including a mistress or "sidechick," may be subject to legal action by a Thai wife under specific conditions.

However, keep in mind that these cases frequently involve several legal considerations and may be more complicated. The wife may be able to recover damages from the third party through a civil lawsuit, including loss of income or emotional distress brought on by the affair. Claims for damages for the diminished value of the marriage or the loss of the husband's financial support may fall under this category. (Thai law, Tuesday, April 16, 2024)

It can be difficult to establish liability and calculate damages in these situations, though. Furthermore, a number of factors, such as the details of the affair, any relevant proof, and the courts' interpretation of Thai law, may affect how these lawsuits turn out.

Thai Marriage Visa

As one of Southeast Asia's top-rated destinations for retirement, job opportunities, and long-term residency, Thailand has drawn an increasing number of foreigners in the last few years. So, it's not unusual for foreigners to marry Thai women after meeting their right ones. The couple's final goal is to stay in Thailand together, and a Thai marriage visa will be required for non-Thais to do so.

A Thai marriage visa may be applied for a foreigner who marries a Thai citizen. Similar to the Non-Immigrant Visa "B" or Non-"B" for work, this one is only granted to those with Thai partners or wives who are Thai citizens.

The Non-O" or Non-Immigrant Visa is the general term for this particular type of visa. Spouses of Thai citizens are eligible to apply for a Thai spouse visa, but only if they meet specific requirements. (Siam Legal International, 2024b)

Note that keep yourself updated about these information overtime.

How a Foreigner Can Buy a Property in Thailand?

Foreigners can directly own a condominium unit but the whole building must have at least 51% Thai ownership.

Partial Ownership of any building can be allowed by buying part of a building (less than 49%) but not the land it is built on. Furthermore, land, house and villas are prohibited.

However, there are alternatives which are creating a Thai Limited Company or a leasehold agreement. Also, a foreigners cannot co-own land, even if married to a Thai citizen. (Bambooroutes, January 7, 2024)

Any foreigner who has been given permission to enter Thailand may purchase a condominium, which is normally a freehold property. Nationality is not a barrier. Buying a condo in Thailand is a fairly easy process that just needs a few things to be in order: A portion of the 49% of the project's surface that is available for foreign ownership must be made up of the acquired property. You can easily confirm this by having a direct conversation at the developer's office with the responsible legal representative. Under the Condo Act, Section 19, foreign ownership is regulated and limited to no more than 49% of the total floor space of all units in a condo building. (Bambooroutes, January 7, 2024)

If you are a foreign investor looking for a condominium in Thailand, you have to check that the building's agreement permits foreign ownership. The project must be registered in accordance with the Condominium Act. This is immediately verified by the Land Office. Funds from outside Thailand must be transferred to buy the condo; that is, the money must come from your foreign account and be converted to Thai Baht. It is necessary to have an official bank statement, sometimes referred to as a "Foreign Exchange Transaction Form," or FET form. Without this documentation, you will not be able to register your name with the condo. Note that keep yourself updated about these regulations overtime.

CONCLUSION

I'm wishing readers luck as they work to develop happy, healthy relationships with Thai girls. As you come to an end of this exploration of cross-cultural relationships between Western men and high-value Thai girls, pause to consider the experiences and growth you have both gained. It is not simple to connect with someone across socio-cultural barriers, but it is only through doing so that genuine connection and understanding can be achieved.

We have examined Thai women's qualities, the complexities of Thai culture, social acceptance and the dynamics of cross- cultural relationships. We've cleared up misunderstandings, talked about difficulties, and offered advice on how to build healthy relationships, settle disputes, and promote trust.

Always remember to be thankful for the wonders of human connection and love as you get ready to embark on your own cross-cultural romance. Honor the distinctions between each partner and the special qualities of your partnership.

Treasure the times when you and another person have laughed, understood, and grown together.

Above all, we live in the world telling us what to value or what "high value woman" looks like. And we need to reflect on what high value is to us. What's the kind of love that aligns with what I value or with what I care about? Because so many people follow the lists that people do have or they're just in their minds, so much of what's on that list is about ego, and it's not about what makes us happy.

"May you find your 'high value Thai woman' who makes you happy and celebrate the connection."

REFERENCES

Bambooroutes (January 7, 2024). Buying a property in Thailand as a foreigner: a complete guide, Retrieved from https://bambooroutes.com/blogs/news/thailand- real-estate-foreigner

Jitkaew, M. N., & Omphornuwat, K. (2019). STEM Pathways: How Thai Culture and Gender Stereotypes Affect Female Career Experiences In STEM Occupations (Doctoral dissertation, Thammasat University).

Kepner, S. F. (2023). The Lioness in bloom: modern Thai fiction about women (Vol. 9). University of California Press.

Kuppako , D. (2014). The Buddhist Cultures in Thai Society: Happy and Harmonious Society . Journal of MCU Social Science Review, 3(3), 92–119. Retrieved from https://so03.tci-thaijo.org/index.php/jssr/article/view/245380

Malikhao, P. (2017). Culture and communication in Thailand (Vol. 3). Singapore:: Springer.

Moussa, M., Doumani, T., McMurray, A., Muenjohn, N., & Deng, L. (2022). Western Culture Meets Eastern Culture: The Thailand Context. In Cross-Cultural Performance Management: Transcending Theory to a Practical Framework (pp. 37- 51). Cham: Springer International Publishing.

Punyapijore C., & Morrison M. A. (2007). Behind the Smile: Reading Cultural Values in Thai Advertising. Asian Journal of Communication, 17(3), 318-336. doi: 10.1080/01292980701458406

Remya, R., & Arasu, B. (2017). Glass Ceiling and Women Employees in Asian Organizations: A Tri- decadal Review. Asia-Pacific Journal of Business Administration, 9(2). DOI: 10.1108/ APJBA-03-2017-0023

Siam Legal International (2024a). Thailand Marriage, Retrieved from https://www.siam-legal.com/thailand-visa/Thailand-Marriage-Visa.php

Siam Legal International (2024b). Marriage Visa Thailand, Retrieved from https://www.siam-legal.com/thailand-visa/Thailand-Marriage-Visa.php

Sodha, B., Özbilgin, M., & Connolly, S. (2010). The Relations between Gender Difference and Advancement in Thai Academic Career. GMSARN International Journal, 4(4), 171-176.

Somswasdi, V. (2003). The Women's Movement and Legal Reform in Thailand.

Thai law (Tuesday, April 16, 2024,). Adultery in Thailand: A Risky and Prohibited Practice, Retrieved from https://www.thailand-business-news.com/law/103579- adultery-in-thailand-a-risky-and-prohibited-practice

Tomasetto, C., Alparone, F. R., & Cadinu, M. (2011). Girlsls math performance under stereotype threat: The moderating role of mothers gender stereotypes. Developmental Psychology, 47(4), 943–949. DOI:10.1037/a0024047

www.ingramcontent.com/pod-product-compliance
Lightning Source LLC
LaVergne TN
LVHW052057160826
845678LV00015B/3269